For Bob, Rob, and Kathryn, thank you for your love and support these past two years. For Mom and Dad, thanks for your encouragement. For my friends, thanks for your excitement!

In memory of Dorothy Coleman Alfriend, my grandmother who always taught me to be myself.

Badges, Egg Salad, and Green Jackets

The MASTERS A to Z

Julie Alfriend Ferris

Illustrated by Joshua Henry Thomas

A Augusta National Golf Club

The Augusta National Golf Club is located in Augusta, Georgia, and hosts the Masters Golf Tournament each year. The club was founded by golfers Bobby Jones and Clifford Roberts. The first Masters was held in 1934. The Augusta National is one of the world's most famous golf courses.

B Badges

Badges are issued to a limited number of people and are used to get into the Tournament on Thursday, Friday, Saturday, and Sunday. Once you are on the list to purchase series badges, you may use them yourself or lend them to friends.

C Clubhouse

The white Clubhouse at Augusta National was built in 1854. It is three stories high. The champions' locker room is inside the Clubhouse. That is where the past champions keep their belongings during the Tournament. The other players use the members' locker room.

D Dogwoods

Many dogwood trees are in full bloom during the Masters. They are small native trees with pretty white or pink blossoms. Azaleas also typically bloom during the Masters. They are shrubs that have white, pink, or red blossoms.

E

Egg Salad Sandwiches

Egg Salad, Pimento Cheese, and Masters Club are popular sandwiches that the patrons look forward to eating while they are at the Tournament. Concession stands provide sandwiches, drinks, chips, and cookies.

F
First Full Week in April

The Masters is held the first full week in April every year and signifies the beginning of spring. People travel to Augusta from many different cities, states, and countries to attend the Masters. The Masters is the first of four major golf tournaments each year.

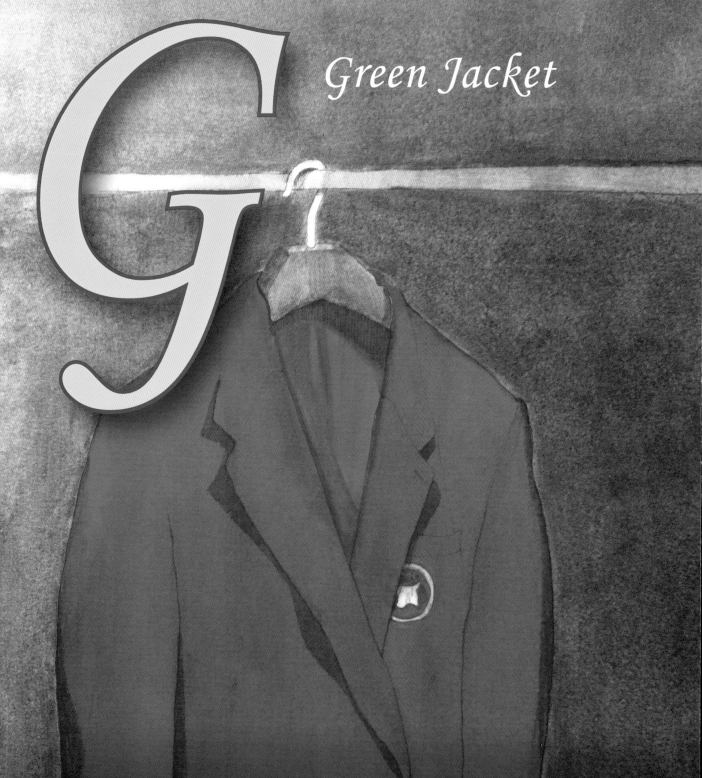

G
Green Jacket

The Green Jacket is worn by members and is presented to the champion in the Butler Cabin immediately following the Tournament. He keeps this jacket for a year and then brings it back to the club when he returns for the Tournament. It is kept in the Clubhouse and he can wear it when he visits.

H Honorary Starters

ARNOLD PALMER
GARY PLAYER
JACK NICKLAUS

Legendary golfers are named Honorary Starters each year. They have typically been past champions who do not compete in the Tournament. They start off the Tournament on Thursday morning by teeing off on hole Number 1. The late Arnold Palmer, Jack Nicklaus, and Gary Player have all been Honorary Starters.

I Ike

General Dwight D. Eisenhower (Ike) was a former United States president as well as an Augusta National Golf Club member. He has a pond and cabin named for him. There was a pine tree named for him on hole Number 17, but it had to be removed in 2014 due to an ice storm that damaged most of the tree's branches. Ike visited Augusta five times before he was president, twenty-nine times while he was president, and eleven times after he left office.

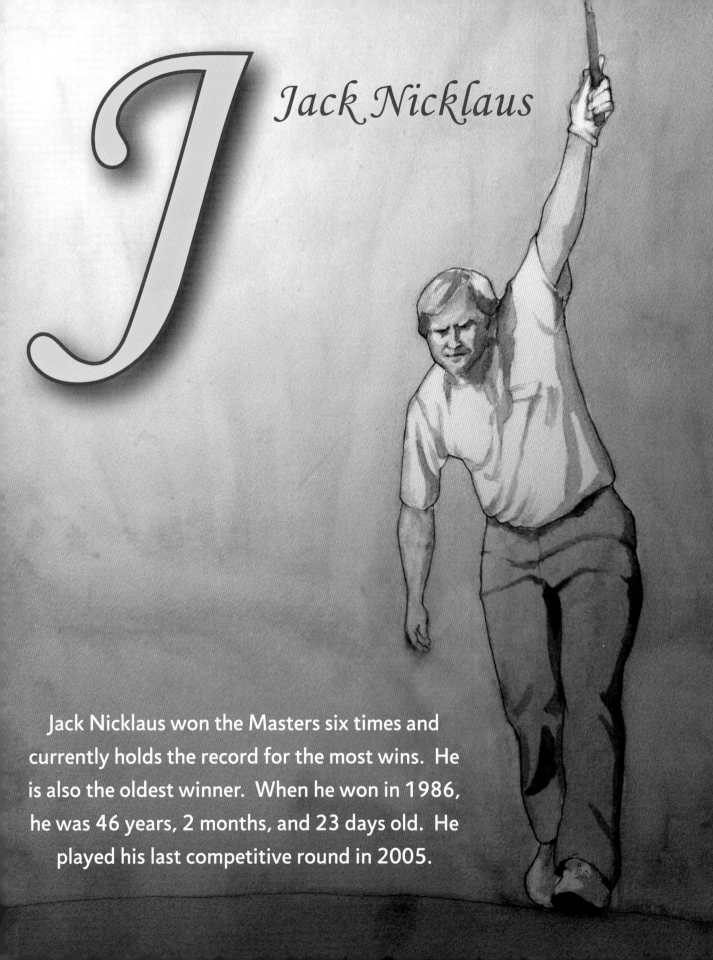

J

Jack Nicklaus

Jack Nicklaus won the Masters six times and currently holds the record for the most wins. He is also the oldest winner. When he won in 1986, he was 46 years, 2 months, and 23 days old. He played his last competitive round in 2005.

K Kids

Kids ages eight to sixteen are allowed to attend the Masters for free through the Junior Pass Program as long as they are with a series badge holder. The badge holder is allowed to bring one junior a day for all four days. Kids also have the opportunity to compete in the Drive, Chip and Putt Championship at Augusta National the Sunday before Masters week. The first Drive, Chip and Putt Championship took place in April 2014.

L Loblolly and Longleaf Pines

Loblolly and Longleaf pine trees line the fairways at Augusta National. Some of the trees were grown there, while others were transplanted to the course. Players often have to hit shots over or around these towering pines.

M

Magnolia Lane

The road that leads from Washington Road to the Clubhouse is Magnolia Lane. Magnolia trees that are over 150 years old line the road on either side. Magnolia Lane was first paved in 1947.

No Cell Phones or Cameras During the Tournament

Cell phones and cameras are not allowed on the course during the Tournament. They are loud and can distract the players when they are hitting the ball. Cameras are allowed only during the Practice Rounds on Mondays, Tuesdays, and Wednesdays.

Official Score Card

An official score card has to be signed by the players after the completion of each round. On Sunday, after the champion has signed the official score card, he proceeds to the Butler Cabin where he is presented with his Green Jacket.

OFFICIAL SCORE

HOLE	1	2	3	4	5	6	7	8	9	Out	10	11	12	13
YARDAGE	445	575	350	240	455	180	450	570	460	3725	495	505	155	510
PAR	4	5	4	3	4	3	4	5	4	36	4	4	3	5
R	5	4	4	3	3	3	4	5	4	35	4	4	4	4

Signature

Attest

P Patrons

Patrons are people who attend the Masters. Most patrons are golf fans who appreciate the competition and beauty of the Augusta National Golf Club. They cheer for their favorite players and also pull for others to do well.

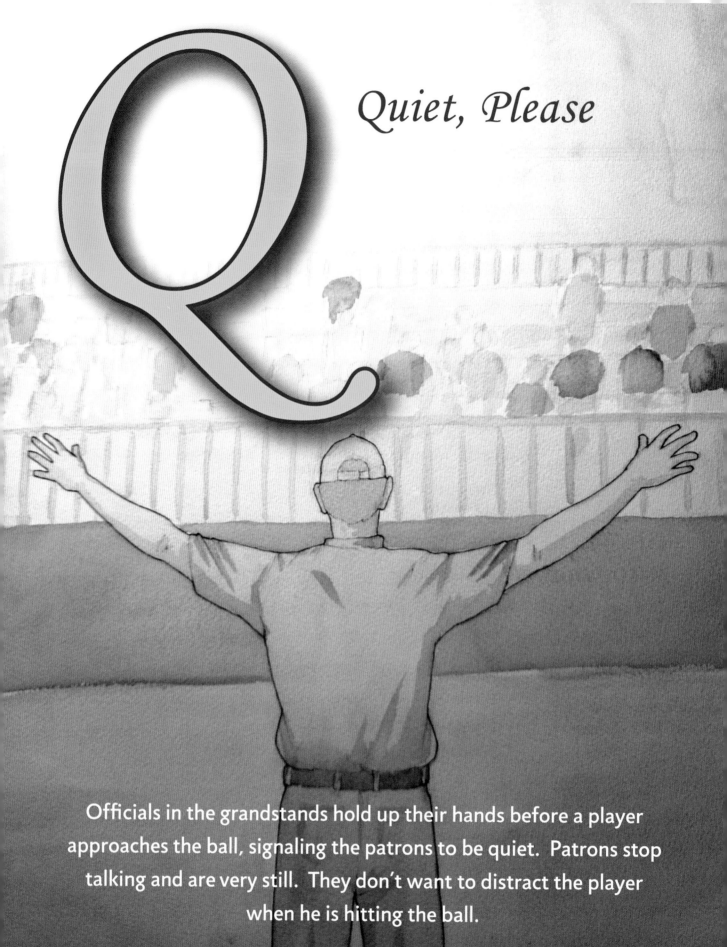

Q

Quiet, Please

Officials in the grandstands hold up their hands before a player approaches the ball, signaling the patrons to be quiet. Patrons stop talking and are very still. They don't want to distract the player when he is hitting the ball.

Rae's Creek

Rae's Creek runs by holes Number 11 and Number 12. A tributary of the creek runs through hole Number 13. Rae's Creek is named after John Rae, who owned a house on the property which is now the Augusta National. These three holes are referred to as Amen Corner. They are some of the most popular holes for patrons to watch.

S

Sarazen

Gene Sarazen had one of the most famous shots during the Masters. In 1935, he had a double eagle on hole Number 15 which helped him win the Masters that year. A double eagle is a 2 on a par 5. This shot has been called, "the shot heard 'round the world."

T Trophy

A trophy that looks like the Augusta National Clubhouse is given to the Masters champion. The permanent silver trophy, the one that stays in the Clubhouse, has the names of the champions engraved on it. The champion takes home a smaller version of the permanent one.

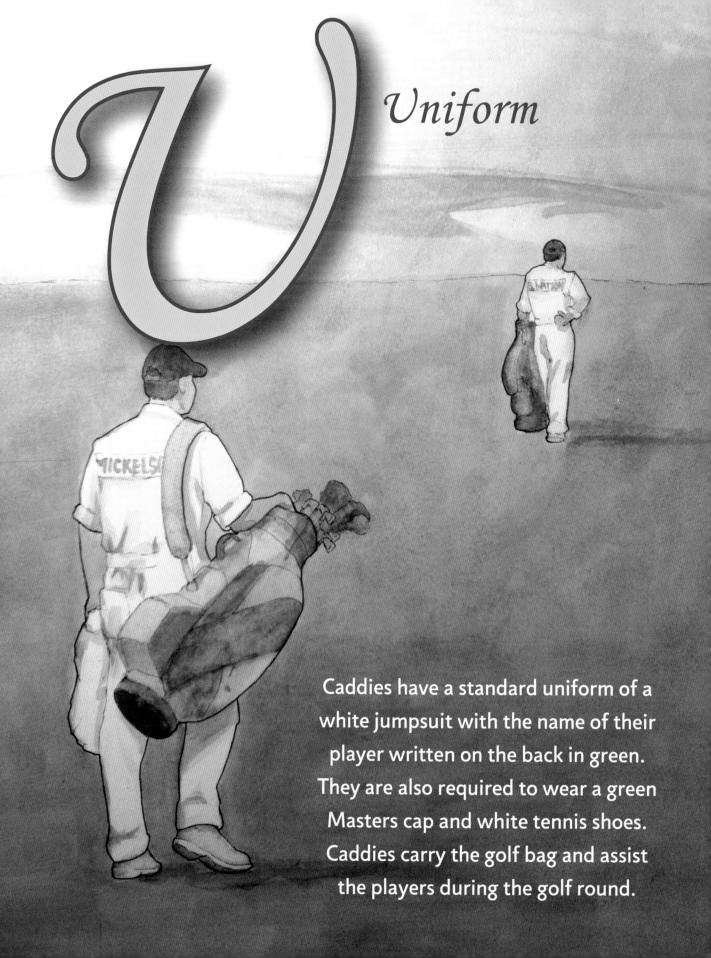

U Uniform

Caddies have a standard uniform of a white jumpsuit with the name of their player written on the back in green. They are also required to wear a green Masters cap and white tennis shoes. Caddies carry the golf bag and assist the players during the golf round.

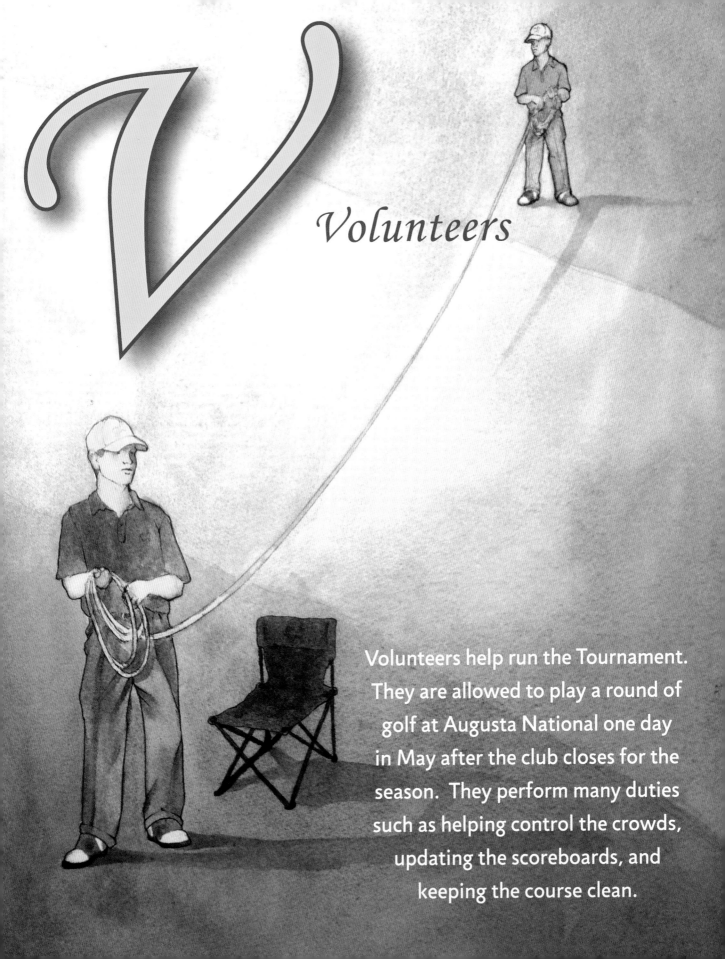

V Volunteers

Volunteers help run the Tournament. They are allowed to play a round of golf at Augusta National one day in May after the club closes for the season. They perform many duties such as helping control the crowds, updating the scoreboards, and keeping the course clean.

W

www.masters.com

www.masters.com is the official website for the Masters. Take a look at it to see the beautiful pictures of the course and learn more information about the players. It also provides a leader board as well as videos during the week of the Tournament.

X

eXtremely Fast Greens

The Augusta National Golf Club is known for fast greens. Bentgrass is grown on the greens and kept closely mowed. Players must be very careful when putting because of the quickness of the greens.

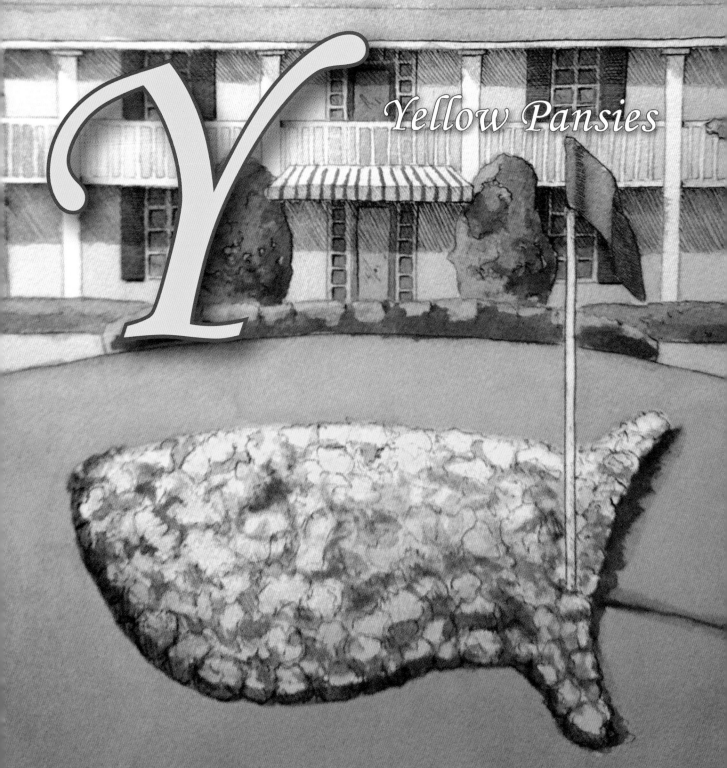

Y

Yellow Pansies

Yellow pansies in the shape of the USA are planted in front of the Clubhouse. A flagstick with a green Masters flag is placed where Augusta is located on the map. Many people stand at this site called Founders Circle to have their picture taken.

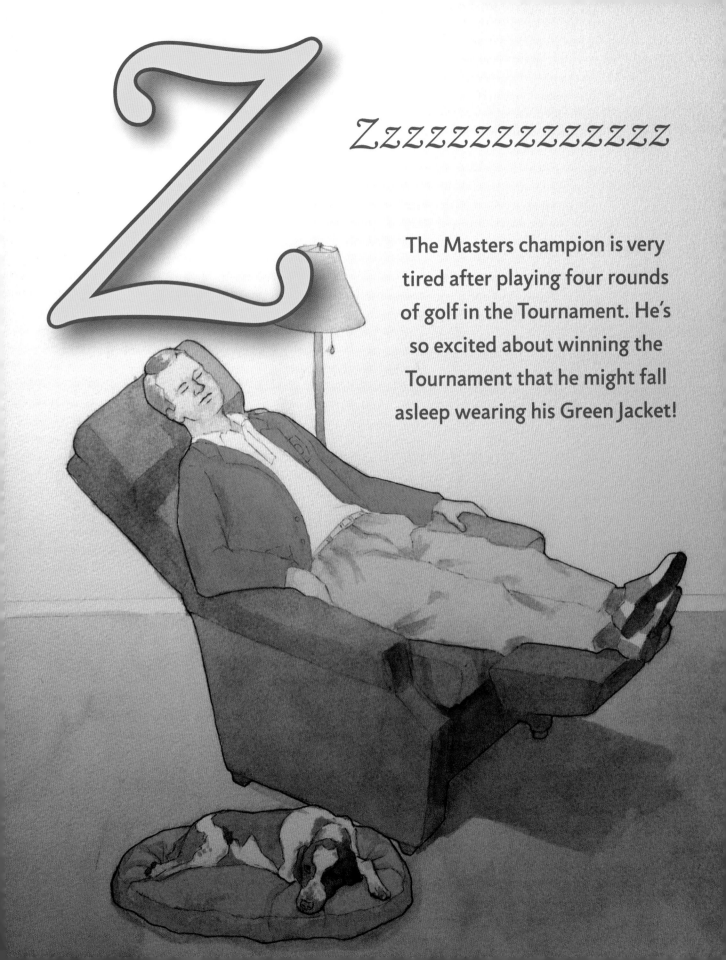

Z

Zzzzzzzzzzzzz

The Masters champion is very
tired after playing four rounds
of golf in the Tournament. He's
so excited about winning the
Tournament that he might fall
asleep wearing his Green Jacket!

The End

Julie is from Thomson, Georgia, and worked at the Masters in high school. She graduated from Georgia Southern University with a degree in Early Childhood Education. From there, she earned her Master's Degree in Early Childhood Education and taught first grade in the Augusta area. Although she doesn't play golf, she enjoys attending the Masters and watching golf on TV. Phil Mickelson is her favorite golfer. Julie currently teaches preschool at her church and lives with her husband and two children in Roswell, Georgia. In her free time, she enjoys activities with her family and playing with her dog, Molly. She loves children's books and believes that reading to children can enrich their lives forever. *The Masters A to Z* is her first children's book. You can visit her website at www.junebugprint.com.

Josh has always wanted to be an artist. He loved to draw and paint growing up and now he favors painting portraits of people. He majored in Painting and minored in Portrait Arts at the Savannah College of Art and Design. Because his dad was a golf coach at Augusta State University, Josh started playing golf at the age of ten and still enjoys playing it when he can. He likes to attend the Masters Tournament where he pulls for his favorite golfers, Bubba Watson and Ian Poulter. Josh helps teach a local golf camp each summer to young children, and when he is not painting or golfing, he loves to fish. Josh lives in Thomson, Georgia, and has a studio in his house.

For Momma and Dad. Thank you for the help and support over the years.

-Josh